Contents

Acknowledgements

Photographs on inside front cover, inside back cover and pages 5, 13, 19, 25, 32(r), 36, 41 courtesy of Empics; pages 3, 11, 27, 29, 30, 31, 35(c), 38 courtesy of Mansoor Ahmed Photography; front cover, back cover and pages 7, 14–18, 20, 32, 35(l+r), 45 and 47 courtesy of Allsport UK. Illustrations by Tim Bairstow of Taurus Graphics.

Note Throughout the book players and officials are referred to individually as 'he'. This should, of course, be taken to mean 'he or she' where appropriate.

1

Equipment

The playing court

Basketball is played on a court marked out on a flat surface. Grass courts are not allowed.

The standard dimensions of the court are 28 m (91 ft 6 in) long and 15 m (49 ft 3 in) wide. Variations of minus 2 m (6 ft 6 in) in length and 1 m (3 ft 3 in) in width are permitted.

The playing court is marked by lines which are clearly visible and 5 cm (2 in) in width.

The baskets

The baskets consist of rings and nets, one at each end of the playing court.

The ring is constructed from solid iron, 45 cm (18 in) in diameter and painted orange.

Nets are best made of white cord suspended from the rings and constructed so that they check the ball momentarily as it passes through the basket.

The ring is attached to the backboards in a horizontal plane and fixed 3.05 m (10 ft) above the floor.

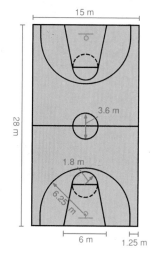

▲ *Fig. 1   Standard playing court*

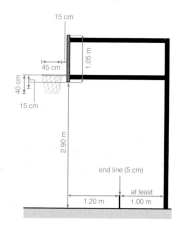

▲ *Fig. 2   Basket, backboard and support*

The backboards

The backboards were originally installed to prevent the ball going out of play and also to stop spectators interfering with shooting. They are now standard equipment required by the rules.

A backboard measures 1.8 m x 1.05 m (6 ft x 3.5 ft) and is usually made of smooth hard wood or a suitable transparent material, 3 cm (1.2 in) thick.

The ball

The ball is spherical and is made of a rubber bladder covered with a case of leather, rubber or synthetic material. It must be between 74.9 cm (29.5 in) and 78 cm (30.7 in) in circumference, with a weight of at least 567 g (20 oz) and not more than 650 g (23 oz).

When inflated and dropped on to a solid wooden floor from a height of about 1.8 m (6 ft), it should rebound to a height of at least 1.2 m (4 ft) and not more than 1.4 m (4.7 ft), measured to the top of the ball.

For a match the home team should provide at least one good used ball. Neither team may use the match ball for warm-up.

Clothing

The individual player's equipment is comparatively simple, the basic playing clothing being shorts and a vest. The player will usually be provided with his vest and shorts by the club, so that members of the team wear identical kit.

Each player must wear numbers on his vest, the one on the front 10 cm (4 in) high and the one on the back 20 cm (8 in) high. Numbers for international play range from 4 to 15. In addition, numbers 20–25, 30–35, 40–45 and 50–55 may be used in some local competitions.

Footwear is a very important part of the player's equipment. Basketball shoes are either low cut or high cut, depending on the personal preference of the player. Shoes should fit well and have a sole thick enough to cushion the strain of the jumping and landing that will occur in the game.

The game

The aim of each team is to throw the ball into its opponents' basket and to prevent the other team from securing the ball or scoring.

The game is started by a 'jump ball' (also known as a 'tip off') at the centre when the referee throws the ball up between two opposing players.

When the ball is in play it may be passed, thrown, rolled, batted or dribbled in any direction. Both passing and/or dribbling are used to move the ball into a scoring position.

The game is stopped when certain rules are infringed. There are four important aspects of play controlled by the rules. These concern:

- contact
- progressing with the ball
- dribbling
- certain time rules.

Basketball, like other games, has rules concerning the method of starting play, restarting after a score and after a violation of the rules.

The court is divided by a half-way line. That half of the court which contains the opponents' basket is referred to as a team's 'front court'. The other half of the court, at the team's defensive end, is its 'back court'.

The game is divided into four quarters of 10 minutes each, with a half-time interval of ten minutes. The game watch is stopped when the whistle is blown, so no playing time is lost during stoppages.

A game cannot end in a draw. An extra period of five minutes is played, plus as many extra periods as are necessary to break the tie.

The teams

The game is played by two teams. Each team can consist of up to ten players, five players from each team being on court during the match. The other players are substitutes and can be used at certain times in the game (*see* page 14).

Each team has a coach who is responsible for:

- his team's tactical play
- supplying the names and numbers of the players to the scorer before the match
- instructing a substitute to report to the scorer when he decides to request a substitution.

Starting play

Play is started by a jump ball (tip off) at the centre circle.

Jump ball

One member of each team stands in the circle, on either side of the line marked across the circle.

All other players must remain outside the restraining circle until the ball has been touched by one of the jumpers.

The referee tosses the ball up between the two players to a height greater than the players can reach by jumping. After the ball has reached its highest point the jumpers may tap it in any direction while it is on its downward flight.

The jumpers may not leave their position until one of them has touched the ball. Neither of them may tap the ball more than twice. The player who has touched the ball twice may not touch it again until it has touched one of the other players, the basket or the backboard.

In play

A player may:

- catch, control, pass or shoot the ball with either or both hands. He must not hit the ball with a clenched fist or deliberately play the ball with his foot, although accidentally striking the ball with the foot or leg is not a violation
- dribble the ball by throwing, batting, bouncing or rolling it. The ball must always touch the floor before the player touches it again. A player is entitled to a dribble each time he gains control of the ball. The dribble ends when he touches the ball with both hands at once or allows it to rest in either or both hands. Having ended the dribble, he may not begin another dribble until he has taken a shot, or the ball has been played by another player
- if the ball was received while standing still, carry it for one complete pace, but not for two or more paces. If the ball was received on the run, a player may carry it for one pace, i.e. a step with one foot and then a step with the other foot, before passing or shooting
- shoot and score from any point in the court
- pivot with the ball held in his hands. That is, he can step once or more in any direction with one foot while turning on the other, which must stay on the floor at its point of contact.

Progression with the ball

When a player wants to advance with the ball he may dribble, i.e. bounce the ball to the ground with one hand.

To stop legally a player must execute the stop within the limits of two steps, one with each foot. The rules specify clearly the limits within which a player may stop and then pivot when carrying the ball. These limits are defined by a two count rhythm, i.e. the step with one foot and then the other. The limits are:

- a player who receives the ball while standing still may pivot using either foot as the pivot foot
- a player who receives the ball while progressing or upon completion of a dribble may use a two count rhythm in coming to a stop or getting rid of the ball. The first count occurs:

(a) as he receives the ball if either foot is touching the floor at the time he receives it, or
(b) as either foot touches the floor or as both feet touch the floor simultaneously after he receives it, if both feet are off the floor when he receives it.

The second count occurs when, after the count of one, either foot touches the floor or both feet touch the floor simultaneously. When a player comes to a legal stop, if one foot is in advance of the other, he may pivot, but only on the one count foot (usually the rear)

- a player who receives the ball while

standing still, or who comes to a legal stop while holding the ball:

(a) may lift the pivot foot or jump when he throws for goal or passes, but the ball must leave his hands before one or both feet again touch the floor (b) may not lift the pivot foot in starting a dribble before the ball leaves his hands.

To progress with the ball in excess of the limits is a violation of the rules.

To play within these rules there are two methods used by players to stop when receiving a pass while moving or when finishing a dribble. These are a 'jump stop' and a 'stride stop'.

Jump stop

To jump stop the player takes the ball in the air and stops, landing on both feet simultaneously.

Stride stop

To stride stop the player uses a full pace to stop. Having caught the ball when both feet are off the ground, the player lands on one foot and then steps forwards on the other.

Time rules

24 seconds

A team in control of the ball must make a try for the basket within 24 seconds of having gained control.

Eight seconds

When a team gains control of the ball in its back court, it must cause the ball to go into the front court within eight seconds.

A player must not cause the ball to go into his team's back court when he is in the front court. This restriction applies to all situations including the throw-in from out-of-bounds, rebounds and interceptions. It does not apply, however, to the situation when a team has a throw-in from out-of-bounds from the mid-point on the side line, following a coach technical foul (*see* page 12) or an unsportsmanlike foul (*see* page 11).

Five seconds

On a throw-in from out-of-bounds a player must throw, bounce or roll the ball to another player in the court within five seconds. When the ball has been placed at the disposal of a player to attempt a free throw (*see* page 13), he must throw the ball within five seconds. The five seconds count is started when the ball is at the disposal of the player and finishes when he releases the ball or the whistle is blown because he has exceeded the five seconds.

When any single player who is closely guarded is holding the ball and does not pass, shoot, bat, roll or dribble the ball within five seconds, this is a violation and the ball is awarded to the opposing team.

Three seconds

A player shall not remain in his opponents' restricted area for more than three seconds when he or his team has control of the ball. This restriction is in force for all out-of-bounds situations, but does not apply while the ball is in the air on a try for goal or during the rebound from the backboard. Allowance may be made for a player who has been in the restricted area for less than three seconds and dribbles in to shoot for goal.

Fouls

A personal foul is a player foul which involves contact with an opponent. A technical foul is an infringement against the spirit of the rules or the use of unsportsmanlike tactics.

Personal fouls

It is the duty of every player on court to avoid contact. If contact occurs a personal foul can be awarded against the player whom the official considers to be primarily responsible.

Every player on court is entitled to occupy any part of the court not occupied by an opponent, provided that he does not cause any personal contact in obtaining that position. A player is considered to occupy not only the part of the floor covered by his feet, but, in addition, a 'cylinder' between the floor and the roof with a base roughly equivalent to the player's body dimensions. Should an opponent run or reach into this cylinder and cause contact, then he is responsible for that contact. If the player, in extending his arm or leg outside his cylinder, causes contact, then he is responsible for that contact. It is legal for a player to extend his arm or leg, but should an opponent wish to move by, then the extended limb must be withdrawn.

The mere fact that the defensive player is attempting to play the ball does not justify him in making contact with the player in possession of the ball. If the defensive player causes personal contact in an attempt to get at the ball from an unfavourable position, he should be penalised.

When players are stationary it is relatively easy for a referee to make a correct judgement as to which player is responsible for any contact that may occur. But it is more difficult when the players are moving. The rules of the game differentiate between a dribbler and a player who does not have the ball. A dribbler is expected to be in full control and be able to stop, change direction, pass or shoot in a split second. A dribbler should expect that defenders will move into his path at any time and should be prepared to take any action necessary to avoid contact. Until the dribbler gets his head and shoulders past the opponent, the greater responsibility for contact remains with the dribbler. Contact by a dribbler on the front of the defensive player will usually result in the foul being called on the dribbler. Should the contact be by the defender on the side of the dribbler, then the foul should be called on the defensive player. Providing the defender can establish a legal defensive position (i.e. with both feet on the floor, facing the dribbler, in the path of the movement of the dribbler), then should contact occur the dribbler is responsible for this contact. Once the defensive position is established, the dribbler must be prepared to avoid contact. A defender, providing he has gained his position first, does not have to give the dribbler time and distance in which to stop.

When defending against a player who does not have the ball, the defender must give a moving opponent time and distance (neither less than one nor more than two paces) in which to stop or change direction. A player must not move into the path of an opponent without the ball so quickly that he cannot stop or change direction.

A player may not contact an opponent with his hand, unless such contact is only with the opponent's hand while it is on the ball and is incidental to an attempt to play the ball.

Judgement of personal fouls

The referee, having judged that illegal contact has occurred and blown the whistle, then has to make a judgement as to the severity of the foul. These cover a normal personal foul, an unsportsmanlike foul and a disqualifying foul.

- The normal personal foul can be looked upon as a mistake by the player, an error in skill that caused the contact.
- An unsportsmanlike foul is contact that results when a player makes no effort to avoid contact, when he intentionally disregards the ball and causes personal contact.
- A disqualifying foul is a flagrant unsportsmanlike foul, e.g. a punch.

In addition, the official has to decide if the foul was committed on a player in the act of shooting or not.

A double foul is a situation where two opponents commit personal fouls against each other at approximately the same time.

Penalty for personal foul

When an official blows his whistle for a personal foul, he indicates the player who has committed the foul. This player has the foul charged against him, i.e. it is recorded on the score sheet. The official moves to a position where he is visible to the scorer and then signals the number of the offender, the nature of the foul, and the penalty that is to follow.

A player who has committed five fouls, personal or technical, must leave the court.

The foul is charged against the offender, plus the following additional penalties.

- **Normal personal foul** The non-offending team is given the ball for a throw-in from out-of-bounds at the side line nearest the site of the foul. However, when a team has committed four player fouls, either personal or technical, in a quarter, all fouls committed are penalised by one plus one free throw (unless the team committing the foul is in control of the ball, in which case the penalty is the same as before the four fouls had been committed).
- **Foul on a player in the act of shooting** If the goal is made, it shall count (two or three points) and, in addition, one free throw shall be awarded. If the goal is missed, two or three free throws shall be awarded.

● **Unsportsmanlike and disqualifying fouls** Two free throws are awarded to the non-offending team except when a goal is scored by the offended player (*see* page 10). After the free throws, whether successful or not, the ball is put into play at mid-court side line by a member of the free thrower's team. For a disqualifying foul the player must leave the game and playing area immediately.

● **Double fouls** No free throws are awarded and the ball is brought into play at the nearest circle by a jump ball between the two players involved.

Technical fouls

Technical fouls are offences against the spirit of the game, but some, which are obviously unintentional and have no effect on the play, or are of an administrative nature, are not considered technical fouls unless they are repeated after a warning by an official. Technical infringements which are deliberate, or unsportsmanlike, or which give the offender an unfair advantage, are penalised immediately with a technical foul.

A player shall not disregard warnings by an official or commit unsportsmanlike actions such as:

• delaying the game by preventing the ball from being put promptly into play
• baiting an opponent or obstructing the opponent's vision by waving his hands close to the opponent's eyes
• using profanities or disrespectfully addressing an official
• changing his number without informing the scorer and the referee
• entering the court as a substitute without reporting first to the scorer and then to an official
• grasping the ring in a manner that may damage the equipment.

Penalty for a player technical foul

Each offence will be charged as a foul against the offender and one free throw plus possession of the ball at half court will be awarded to the opponents. The captain shall designate the thrower. For infringements that are persistent or flagrant a player shall be disqualified.

Technical foul by coach or substitute

The coach, assistant coach or substitute must stay within their team bench area and may not enter the court without permission. Neither may they leave their places to follow the action on the court nor disrespectfully address officials (including table officials) or opponents.

Here again a distinction is made between unintentional and deliberate infringements.

During a charged time-out (*see* page 15) a coach may address his players, including substitutes. The coach may also direct and encourage his team during the game from the bench.

Penalty for a coach/ substitute technical foul

Each offence by a coach, assistant coach or substitute shall be recorded and two free throws awarded to the opponents. After the free throws, whether successful or not, the ball is put into play at mid-court side line by a member of the free thrower's team. Persistent or flagrant infringements may cause the coach to be banished from the vicinity of the court. The assistant coach or, if none, the captain, would then replace him.

Free throws

A free throw for a personal foul is awarded to the player who was fouled, unless he is disqualified for any reason, or injured. To take the free throw the thrower stands immediately behind (not on) the free throw line.

Nobody – not even an official – may stand inside the free throw lane when a player is taking a free throw. The other players may line up along the sides of the lane, in the spaces marked, during a free throw (except following a technical foul or an unsportsmanlike or disqualifying foul). The spaces nearest the basket are for two players of the defending team, with the other players taking alternate positions.

The free thrower is allowed a maximum of five seconds to take his shot. The thrower may not touch the line or the floor in the free throw lane until the ball touches the ring or until it is apparent that it will not touch it. However, the players lining up along the side of the free throw lane may move across the line as soon as the ball is released by the free thrower.

After a team has committed four player fouls, personal or technical, in a quarter, when a player of the team not in control of the ball commits a subsequent foul, the player against whom the foul has been committed is given two free throws.

Substitutions

Any or all of the five players in action may be replaced by substitutes during the game. Substitutions are made on instructions by the team's coach. The coach should send the substitute – who must be ready to play – to the scorer. After reporting to the scorer, the substitute must sit on the seat provided until the scorer sounds his signal. He should then stand up and indicate to the nearest floor official that he wishes to enter the court. He should not enter the court until beckoned to do so by an official, whereupon he should enter the court immediately.

Substitutions can only be made when the ball is 'dead' and the game clock has been stopped.

Following a violation, only the team which has possession of the ball for the throw-in from out-of-bounds may effect a substitution. If this occurs the opponents may effect a substitution.

Both teams may substitute when a foul or a jump ball is called, but, should the team wish to substitute when free throws have been awarded, this must take place before the first throw is taken. The player taking the free throw may be substituted provided the request was made before the first throw and that his last throw was successful. In this case, the opponents may be granted one substitution.

If a player is injured and in danger the officials can stop the game immediately. Otherwise the officials wait until the play has been completed (i.e. the team in possession of the ball has thrown for goal, has withheld the ball from play, or the ball has become 'dead') before the game is stopped. If the injured player cannot continue to play, he shall be substituted within one minute, and the substitute takes any free throws or his place at the jump ball.

Charged time-out

A charged time-out may be granted to each team during each quarter of playing time, with two in the final quarter and one charged time-out for each extra period.

A time-out is of up to one minute's duration and gives an opportunity for the coach to change tactics and give instructions to his players.

A request for a charged time-out can be granted when the ball is 'dead' and the game clock is stopped, or following a field goal (*see* page 19) scored by the opponents of the team that has made the request.

Out-of-bounds

The ball is out-of-bounds:

• when it touches a player who is out-of-bounds, i.e. a player touching the floor on or outside the boundary line, and that player is held responsible
• when it touches any other person, the floor or any object on or outside the boundary, or the supports or back of the backboard. It is considered to have been put out-of-bounds by the player who last touched it.

An official then indicates the team which is to put the ball into play. A player from this team standing out-of-bounds, on or behind the boundary line near where the ball left the court, must, within five seconds from the time the ball is at his disposal, throw, bounce or roll it to another player within the court, from out-of-bounds at the boundary line near where the ball left the court.
When the ball is awarded to a team

out-of-bounds, an official must hand the ball to the player who is to put it in play. This is to clarify the decision and not delay the game.
While the ball is being passed into the court, every other player must be completely inside the court.
Note – if the ball goes out-of-bounds

(a) after being touched simultaneously by two opponents
(b) and the official is in doubt as to who last touched it
(c) and the officials disagree

play is restarted by a jump ball between the two players concerned for (a), and for any two opponents for (b) and (c) at the nearest restraining circle.
When the ball is awarded out-of-bounds at the end line following a violation or infraction to the rules, the ball is thrown in from the nearest point to the infraction, except directly behind the backboard.

Held ball

A held ball may be declared:

• when two or more rival players of opposing teams have one or both hands firmly on the ball, so that neither of them can get it away without using 'undue roughness'
• when the ball lodges in the basket supports.

After calling a held ball, the referee then orders a jump ball. This takes place at the centre of the nearest restraining circle.

Restarting play

The method of starting play after fouls and held balls has been described earlier. For other violations of the rules the ball is awarded to the non-offending team for a throw-in from the nearest point at the boundary line out-of-bounds.

After a field goal, play is restarted by an opponent of the scoring team by throwing the ball into court from behind the end line where the goal was scored.

Scoring

Two or three points are awarded for a goal from the field, i.e. when the ball enters the basket from above as a result of ordinary play. Two points will normally be awarded for a field goal, unless the shot is taken from outside the marked semi-circle (6.25 m/20.5 ft from the basket), when three points are awarded.

One point is awarded for a goal by a free throw.

If a team refuses to continue to play after being so ordered by the referee, it forfeits the game. The opponents are credited with a 2–0 win unless they were leading at the time of forfeit, when the score stands.

If a defensive player touches the ball when it is on its downward flight during a shot for basket, or touches the ring or backboard while the ball is on the ring during a try for goal, or the basket when the ball is in the basket, this is interference and the shooter will be awarded a goal for his shot.

Control of the game

Officials

The officials are a referee and an umpire, who are assisted by a scorer and a timekeeper and, in top-class games, a shot clock operator.

The referee and umpire are required to wear a uniform of long black trousers, a grey shirt and black sports shoes.

The referee and umpire jointly conduct the game according to the rules. Their duties include:

● putting the ball into play
● stopping play when the ball is 'dead'
● ordering time-out
● beckoning substitutes onto the court
● passing the ball to a player for a specified throw from a prescribed position
● silently counting seconds to administer certain time rules (*see* page 8).

The officials are responsible for imposing penalties for breaches of the rules and for unsportsmanlike conduct.

Play is stopped by one of the officials blowing a whistle when a decision has to be made known, usually through the use of an official signal.

The referee is the senior official and is responsible for:

● the inspection and approval of all equipment
● tossing the ball at the centre to start play
● deciding whether a goal shall count if the officials disagree
● a team's forfeiture of a game when conditions warrant it
● deciding questions on which the timekeeper and scorer disagree
● examining the score sheet and approving the score at the end of each half
● making decisions on any points not covered by the rules.

The 24-second shot clock is required to operate the device for timing 24 seconds. However, when there is no such device this duty is undertaken by the trailing official (*see* page 22).

Refereeing technique

The basic responsibility of the officials is to have the game played with as little interference as possible on their part. It is the purpose of the rules to penalise a player who by reason of an illegal act has placed his opponents at a disadvantage. To be able to undertake his responsibility a good official (referee or umpire) must:

● know the rules of the game
● be in the right place
● be looking at the right part of the court.

The referee and umpire control the game by a division of duties and by co-operating so that they watch all of the play and all of the players. To do this they use a system of double officiating. The officials work on opposite sides of the court, each official being responsible for the side line nearest to him, and the end line and the free throw lane to his right. Before each jump ball and after each foul, the officials change sides of the court. During normal floor play the officials do not try to keep level with the ball because any quick movement of the ball would leave them both behind play and in a bad position to see what is happening on court.

The officials endeavour to 'sandwich' the ball between them with one always ahead of the play (the 'leading' official) and the other behind the play (the 'trailing' official). During the game each official moves to his right ahead of play (leading) and to his left behind the play (trailing). While play is developing, the leading official will find he is primarily responsible for play away from the ball, e.g. he looks for contact as players manoeuvre for position, and three seconds violations, while the trailing official will find he is

primarily concerned with the ball and the players around it. Each official will blow for and penalise any infringements he sees anywhere on court.

As far as possible the officials should keep off the court and their normal lines of movement to their observation areas should be outside the side and end lines. They may 'cut the corners' as either leading or trailing official if they need to do so, provided they in no way interfere with the movement of the ball or the players on the court. It

is normally only for 'fast breaks' that the officials need to cut the corners in order to keep up with the play. In such cases it is unlikely that there will be anyone in the corners of the court with whom they might interfere. It is permissible for the official to station himself on court if by so doing he can better observe the play and the players. He should do so only while bearing in mind that he must in no way impede the play, and that his normal position is outside the court.

▶ Fig. 3 After the jump ball, play goes to the left. The direction of the movement of the officials to take up 'leading' (green) and 'trailing' (brown) positions is indicated. When play moves to the opposite end of the court, the movement of the officials is indicated by broken lines.

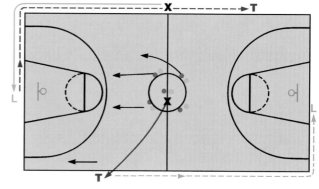

Officials' signals

The officials use a number of hand signals to indicate their decisions to players, the table officials and spectators. These can be found in the official rule book.

The scorer

The scorer's equipment consists of an official score sheet (*see* fig. 4), a signal (horn or bell), five markers numbered 1–5 and two team foul markers.

The scorer is required to:

• record the names and numbers of all players taking part in a game, and inform the nearest official if there is any breach of the rules regarding the numbers and substitution of players
• keep a chronological running summary of the points scored by each team
• note all fouls, personal and technical, and alert an official immediately when a player has committed a total of five fouls, or a team has committed a total of seven fouls
• indicate the number of fouls committed by each player by raising the appropriate numbered marker
• record the time-outs debited to each team, and warn a team through an official when it has taken a second time-out
• sound his signal when a substitution or charged time-out is requested.

The score sheet

The score sheet (*see* fig. 4) consists of three sheets: the original on white paper – this is for the organisers of the match; a copy on pink paper – for the winning team; a copy on gold paper – for the losing team.

In the running score section, the scorer keeps a chronological running summary of the points scored by both teams. There are four columns for keeping the running score. Each column consists of centre spaces with the running score (from 1 to 160). The blank column and a set of running scores to the left are for team A and those on the right are for team B.

When a field goal is scored, the scorer draws a diagonal line over the new running total for the team that has just scored. When a free throw is scored, this is recorded with a darkened circle over the new running score total.

In the blank space on the same side as the new score, the scorer inserts the number of the player who scored the field goal or the free throw.

When a three-point field goal is scored, this is recorded by drawing a circle around the number of the player who scored as well as a diagonal line through the new total.

At the end of a half the scorer draws a heavy darkened circle around the last number of points scored by each team, and a heavy horizontal line under the points scored as well as the number of the player who scored the last points.

Fouls

When a foul (personal or technical) is called against a player, the scorer shall record this in the appropriate square against the players by inscribing a *P* for a personal foul, a *U* for an unsportsman-like foul, a *D* for a disqualifying foul, and a *T* for a technical foul.

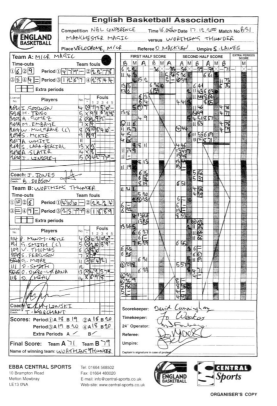

▲ *Fig. 4 Scorer's sheet*

In addition to recording the foul against the player, the scorer will also inscribe a large X inside the box under the team fouls section of the score sheet.

Time-out

When a team requests and is granted a charged time-out, the scorer shall indicate this by marking a large X inside the appropriate space. Both teams are allowed one time-out in each of the first, second and third periods, two time-outs in the fourth quarter and one each in any subsequent periods.

The timekeeper

The timekeeper's equipment consists of two stopwatches (a game watch and a time-out watch), and a signal (gong, horn or bell), which is different from the scorer's signal.

The timekeeper is required to:

• notify the referee more than three minutes before the start of each half, so that the referee can give the teams a

clear three minutes warning before the game is to start
- record playing time
- time stoppages
- indicate the ending of playing time in each half or extra period by sounding his signal.

The game watch is started:

- if play is resumed by a jump ball – when the ball after reaching its highest point is tapped by the first player
- if a free throw is not successful and the ball is to continue in play – when the ball touches a player on the court
- if play is resumed by a throw-in from out-of-bounds – when the ball touches a player on the court.

The game watch is stopped when an official signals a violation, a foul, a held ball, suspension of play for an injury, suspension of play for any reason by an official, or when the 24 second signal sounds.

Playing positions

Basketball is a game of maximum participation; no player on either team is restricted from getting the ball whenever it is in play, and players are free to occupy any part of the playing area not occupied by an opponent. Each player can shoot from any position on the playing court. The popularity of the game can be traced to this essential simplicity, which enables every player to do everything. Although the game is simple to play, to master it requires practice on the part of individual players and the team.

A player's position in the team will depend upon his own skill, that of his team mates, his height in relation to other members of the team and the opponents, and the tactics the coach decides to use. The name given to a player's position is determined by the area of the court usually taken up when the team is attacking. There are three basic court playing positions – guard, forward and centre or post.

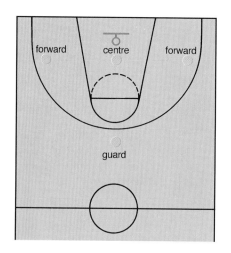

▲ *Fig. 5 Playing positions*

Guard

A player who plays in the guard position will, when his team is on attack, usually operate in the area of the court between the centre line and the free throw line extended to the side lines. He will usually be one of the smaller players on the team and will be responsible for bringing the ball up court to start the team's attack. A talented guard will be able to use his drive to move in close to the basket, not necessarily for a shot, but to draw the defence on to himself and then pass off to a team mate in a better position for the shot.

Forward

The forwards play on attack in the area of the court, either on the right- or left-hand side, between the restricted areas and the side lines. They will be among the taller players on the team, possess a good drive (*see* page 33) and be able to shoot well from the corner and side of the court. If they are playing forward, they must be prepared to move in to gain attacking rebounds should a shot be missed.

Centre or post

The player selected to play in the centre position is usually the tallest player in the team and plays on attack close to the basket. The player in this position is occasionally referred to as a 'post'. A centre or post will be expected to have the following skills:

- be a good shot close to the basket (usually under pressure from close marking opponents)
- have the ability to get free to receive a pass and remain close to the basket
- to rebound strongly.

These playing positions are by no means rigid, and as the team's attacking play develops so a guard may find himself playing from a forward position. However, an inexperienced player will find it easier to understand his role in the team's attack if he learns to operate from these specific court positions.

The number of players that a team uses in each position can be varied, and will depend upon the tactics selected by the coach. The use of players by the coach will ensure a balanced spacing in the front court.

Individual play

The simplest defence used in the game is for a defensive player to be responsible for one opponent, aiming to limit the attacking options of that player. The basic attacking options available to the player are to shoot, to drive (*see* page 33), to pass and to move. (Before using any of these options the attacking player may make use of a fake.) The basic defensive position should be taken up between the attacking player and the basket that is being defended, so that the attacking player has to dribble round the defender in order to take a close range shot. The defender will adjust his position, use his hands to discourage an easy shot or pass, and his feet to prevent a dribbler from penetrating close to the basket.

Attack

Getting free to receive a pass

It must be remembered that a successful pass involves two players – the passer and the receiver. A signal by the potential receiver is vital.

When very closely marked, the attacking player can aim to step across between the defender and the ball. The attacker aims to place one foot in front of the defender's front foot.

If the receiver is marked, a movement will be required to lose the defender. This could be one or a combination of the following movements:

- towards the ball
- away from the ball and then back to receive the ball in the space created by the movement away
- towards the basket and then back to receive the ball
- a change of direction and a change

of speed – in particular, changing speed from slow to fast (walk to run).

Catching

Having moved free, the receiver should:

- make a target with his hands for the passer to aim at
- keep his eyes on the ball
- receive the ball by catching it in two hands with the fingers spread, and cushion it by bending the arms
- endeavour to get the ball under control in two hands as quickly as possible, so he is ready to shoot, start a dribble or make a pass. This is usually called the 'triple threat position'.

Shooting

Once the ball has been caught the attacking player should check if he is within scoring range. To do this may involve him facing the goal, using a pivot immediately the ball is caught so as to look for the basket. If, when he faces the basket, there is no defender in line between him and the basket, he could dribble and use a lay-up shot. Should the attacking player find he is within scoring range and the opponent is not close, but is in position between the ball and basket, the ball handler may use a set shot or a jump shot.

When shooting, a player should be intent to:

• look for the shot early, concentrating on the ring before, during and after the shot
• hold the ball firmly in both hands, fingers spread, with the shooting hand behind and slightly under the ball, and with the fingers pointing up, wrist cocked back. The support hand should be at the side

• shoot the ball upwards with a full extension of the shooting arm in the direction of the basket
• flight the ball with a strong wrist and finger flick, following through with the wrist and fingers in the direction of the shot
• be on balance and under control during the shot; this enables a smooth follow-through which is essential for accuracy. Balance starts at the feet, so always establish a firm foot position, facing the basket, before shooting.

Hook shot If the attacking player is close to the basket but has a defender close by and in a good position, a hook shot can be used. This is similar to a lay-up shot except that the player often starts with his back to the basket, steps so that he has his body between the defender and the basket, and looks over the shoulder for it. The shooter jumps and takes the ball up with two hands using a gentle flick of the wrist and fingers to make the basket.

▲ *Hook shot*

Lay-up shot   The essential ingredients of the shot are that it is taken on the move, usually on the *run*. The player *jumps* up and towards the basket as he shoots, and *stretches* to release the ball as close to the basket as possible.

As the player moves forwards and picks the ball up at the end of a dribble or after receiving a pass, he takes the ball in two hands, lifting his head as he gathers the ball so that he can look for the shot early. The player lands first on his right foot and then on his left foot, as he takes a long final step. This enables him to control his forward momentum and helps him to prepare for the high jump off the left foot. As he jumps off one foot, he carries the ball upwards, still in both hands. The take-off foot for the shot should be opposite the shooting hand. The player releases the ball at full stretch from one hand, using the backboard to bank the ball into the basket.

▲ *Lay-up shot*

Set shot   Although this shot has limited use in the modern game, it may be used for distance shots should the defender sag off, and will be used for free throws. It is also useful for young players to develop this shot. The player making the set shot takes up a stride position with his feet, the same foot forwards as the shooting hand. Prior to taking the shot he bends his knees slightly. The player looks at the basket throughout the shot. The movement starts with a powerful drive from the legs and finishes with the player at full stretch as he follows through with a vigorous snap of the wrist and fingers.

Jump shot This is perhaps the most effective shot in the modern game. It may be taken following a head or foot fake, after a pivot, after receiving a pass, or at the end of a dribble. The player aims to take off from both feet in a vertical direction. As he jumps the ball is taken up in front of his face to a position above the head with the shooting hand behind the ball, just in front of the forehead. The ball is released, near the top of the jump, with an upwards extension of the arm, and flipped towards the basket with a vigorous wrist and finger action.

Dunk shot This is a shot in which a player jumps to put the ball down into the basket. It is similar to a lay-up shot except that the player reaches up with the ball to above the level of the ring (i.e. 3.05 m/10 ft).

▲ *Jump shot*

▲ *Dunk shot*

Footwork

The stride and jump stop have been explained already (*see* page 7). The jump stop is particularly valuable because there is no commitment to a pivot foot on landing. As the landing has been made on both feet simultaneously, either foot may be selected to be the pivot foot, depending on the game situation. A pivot can be used by a player to establish balance, improve his position and create space for a shot.

Stops and the use of pivot should be employed as part of a natural moving action, i.e. as part of a run or walk.

Dribbling

The dribble is an essential skill to develop because it enables the player to move with the ball. The player controls the ball by spreading the fingers comfortably so that they contact as much of the ball as possible. The ball is pushed down firmly using hand, elbow and wrist. The dribbling hand should be on top of the ball. This will prevent 'palming' and ensure that the ball rebounds to hand accurately.

Once the player has mastered the touch of the dribble he must dribble by feel only, so that he can simultaneously see movements by team mates and opponents.

Some inexperienced players fall into the habit of bouncing the ball every time they receive a pass. This prevents another dribble and it limits the individual attacking movements of these players. A skilled player is able to dribble equally well with either hand, to change direction and speed. It is through these manoeuvres that he can beat an opponent. Dribbling the ball towards the basket in an attempt to beat an opponent and take a shot is called a 'drive'.

The drive

The drive will be used by an attacking player to beat a defender who makes a mistake. These are likely to be mistakes in balance in relation to the attacking player and the basket. The main ones are:

● moving towards the attacking player. This is the mistake most commonly made by beginners who, after the man they are marking has received a pass and is facing the basket, rush towards him. In this situation they can be caught off balance easily and beaten with a drive

● jumping up to check an anticipated shot. While the defender is going up, the attacking player can drive round him for the basket

● moving backwards towards the basket. This gives the attacking player time and space for a shot

● movement laterally – left or right. If the defensive player is to the attacker's left, the drive can be made to the right.

To cause the defender to make one of these mistakes a fake may be necessary. For example, a player facing the goal and looking up towards the basket can find that the defender thinks that a shot is about to be taken, and moves accordingly. Movements laterally can be caused by the use of a foot fake before the start of the dribble, or, if the attacking player is already dribbling, by the use of a change of direction and change hands dribble.

A player in a stationary position

facing a close marking opponent is in a good position to use a fake and drive. For example, to move to the right of the opponent the attacker can step to the left with the left foot. As the defender moves to cover the fake, the attacker can step again with the left foot crossing over in front of the opponent, to step past and to drive to the basket. The player uses his right foot as the pivot foot throughout. The fake step should be a short jab step. Remember that the rules require the ball to leave the hand at the start of the dribble, before the pivot foot is lifted.

The ball handler should check which foot the defender has forwards. The defender will find it difficult to move the forward foot back quickly, and the attacking dribble past him should be made down the side of his forward foot.

Passing

To be effective a pass must be taken by the receiver *when* and *where* he wants it and the importance of timing the pass and placing it in relation to the position of the receiver should be stressed. Passing involves two players – the passer and the receiver – and getting free to receive a pass was covered on page 28. The passer must be able to make accurate passes so that the receiver can become an immediate triple threat, i.e. can shoot, drive or pass. A skilled passer should try to be deceptive, disguising his intentions by not staring at the team mate and not 'winding up'. Passes should be quick and firm, with a swift release of the ball preferable to a fast, hard movement through the air. The fast pass that requires a preparatory wind-up will give the opponents a chance to anticipate the pass. The passer will also need to appreciate the relative positions and movements being made by opponents and team mates.

The following are the main passes used in the game.

Bounce pass This is a useful pass to use to pass under a taller opponent or a player with his arms up. The pass is similar to the chest pass except that the ball starts from a lower position and is skidded by the passer to the team mate via the floor. One or two hands may be used in making this pass.

Two hand overhead pass This is an excellent pass for the taller player to use when passing over a smaller player. The ball is taken up in two hands to a position above the head and from this position it is passed with a vigorous snap of the wrist and fingers directly to a team mate.

Chest pass This is the most important and basic pass of the game, used for fast accurate passing at short range. From a position with the ball held in two hands at the chest with the fingers alongside the ball and thumbs behind, pass the ball by fully extending the arms, snapping the wrist and pushing the ball with the fingers. Relax the elbows and extend the arms to follow through fully..

Hand-off pass When a team mate is cutting close to the ball handler, a short hand-off pass is used. The ball is put into the air so that the cutting player can take it as soon as possible after the ball leaves the passer's hand.

▲ *Bounce pass*

▲ *Chest pass*

▲ *Two-hand overhead pass*

35

Movement

Once a player has passed the ball he should look for opportunities to move to receive a return pass. One of the basic attacking moves in the game is the 'Give and go'. A player 'gives' – passes the ball to a team mate – then 'goes' – cuts to the basket looking for a return pass.

Give and go Any two players on court can work together in this way, with a player taking advantage of a mistake by his opponent to cut free or make a fake, e.g. a change of direction to beat his opponent. In the game the give and go is usually used either between two guards or, more likely, between a guard and a forward. In this latter move the guard passes ahead to a forward and then cuts for the basket for the return pass.

Playing against an inexperienced defender, the player who passes ahead, as in a guard-to-forward move, may find that the defender is tempted to turn to see where the ball has gone; at this moment the attacking player is free and should immediately cut for the basket, signalling for the return pass. To make the immediate cut, a player needs to be well balanced, with knees flexed so as to be able to make the quick start that will enable the player to get past the opponent. Should the opponent not make an error, it can be forced by using a change of direction and pace to beat him.

Individual play

Defence

A player's responsibility in defence against an opponent with the ball may be listed as follows:

• discourage the opponent from shooting from a high percentage scoring area (*see* page 39)
• anticipate his moves so as to discourage him driving past for a shot from closer to the basket
• make it difficult for the opponent to pass accurately, particularly passes into the high percentage scoring area.

To be able to defend, an individual usually takes a defensive position between the opponent and the basket. If the opponent is in a shooting position, the defender should be close enough to discourage the shot; should the opponent be away from the ball, the defender can sag off him towards the basket he is defending, changing his stance so as to be able to see the opponent and the ball.

To maintain this position the defender needs a stance with knees slightly flexed and head up, feet flat on the floor and spread approximately shoulder width apart, with one foot in front of the other. This stance enables the defender to make quick movements; the footwork used is a sliding action. Try not to cross the feet so that rapid changes of direction can be made.

Good defence is not static: every time an attacking player moves, a defender should move; every time the ball moves, all the defenders should adjust their positions.

The hands and arms play an important part in defence. They can be used to maintain balance and discourage offensive shooting, driving or passing.

Good defence is played with the two ends of the body – the feet and the brain. The defender needs to analyse his opponent's moves, his strengths and his weaknesses, so as to be able to anticipate and reduce the attacking player's potential options. For example, can his opponent only dribble successfully with one hand or does he have a favourite shooting position? If he is a potential pass receiver, then the defender may adjust his position and place a hand in the passing lane to discourage the pass.

Although the basic defensive position when marking the ball handler will be for the defender to stand between the attacking player and the basket, when marking an opponent who does not have the ball an adjustment must be made. The defender marking off the ball moves into position so as to be able to see the opponent and the ball. It will help if the defender points one hand at the ball and the other at the opponent. In addition, the defender marking the ball should move from an in-line position against the opponent to a position nearer to the ball in order to establish a triangle of ball-defender-opponent. The defender standing in this position will find it easier to help cover should a team mate be beaten by an opponent who dribbles or cuts towards the basket.

Blocking-out and rebounding

To create more possession of the ball it is vital for a team to rebound the missed shots. For the attacking team it will provide an opportunity for a second shot; for the defenders to gain the rebound will mean they have a chance to take the ball down court and mount another attack.

The following basics on blocking-out and rebounding should be remembered:

• when the shot goes up the opponent should be located
• look for errors such as turning to watch the ball or getting too far 'under' the backboard

• step towards the opponent and pivot so that a position has been established between the opponent and the back-board
• spread wide with the knees bent
• feel the opponent on the back
• move with the opponent so as to block their path to the ball
• watch the flight of the ball and jump vigorously up towards the ball, using the arms to obtain extra lift.

If the defenders gain the rebound they will look to make a quick pass to a team mate, or dribble out from the crowded under-basket area. If the rebounding player is on attack he may try to tip the ball back into the basket. Should a tip-in be impossible, he should secure the rebound, land and immediately look to jump aggressively straight back up for a shot.

Team play

To achieve the basic aim of the game, both teams play a 'percentage' game. The team on attack endeavour to move the ball to a position from which they will have a high percentage chance of scoring, while the defensive team tries to stop the opponents gaining a position for a good shot, thereby attempting to give the attacking team only the poor percentage shots – the long range shots and those taken by closely marked players.

Team play involves the application of the following concepts.

Safe passing

Tackling is not permitted in the game so a team should find it relatively easy to retain possession of the ball. To do this they must:

- pass and catch with two hands
- use short range passes (3–4 m/ 10–15 ft)
- hold the ball ready prior to the pass – this is usually chest height or above
- discourage the use of long range or lob passes
- ensure the receiver of the pass moves free and signals to his team mate
- have the passer aim to make accurate passes to the front of the receiver
- use fakes to disguise passing intentions.

Spread out

On the limited area of a court, the team on attack should endeavour to spread out so that there is 3–4 m (10–15 ft) between each attacking player. This makes it difficult for one defender to mark two attackers, which in turn facilitates fast, accurate passes and gives space between defenders into which the attackers can move.

Movement and control

The basic attacking play in basketball should be a pass to a team mate and a movement towards the basket, looking for a return pass. Beginners and inexperienced players frequently attempt to play the game too fast and make too much movement. Basketball is a game of changes of tempo; play may be initially built up slowly and then rapid movement is made as a scoring chance is developed.

Since there is no tackling in the game, emphasis should be placed on controlled movements about the court. A player should move only when he has himself and the ball under control.

Attack

The attacking team will aim to convert each possession of the ball into a high percentage shot at basket. Attacking play will be built on individual players working alone, with two players combining to create a scoring opportunity for one of the pair, and occasionally with three attacking players working together.

Although some of the team plays that follow may seem complicated to the complete beginner, they are in essence relatively simple to instigate. First remember that each individual player, when he receives the ball, should check his options – can (or should) he shoot – drive – pass – move?

A simple team tactic could be stated as follows.

• Look ahead – face the basket you are attacking, particularly when you are holding the ball.
• Pass ahead.
• Move ahead – on gaining possession quickly start an attack by moving the ball ahead with a fast break, cut to the basket after a pass, drive to the basket, and get ahead of the team mate holding the ball.
• Spread out, so as to keep space between team mates and to leave the under-basket area clear.
• Control – most of the game is played without the ball, so move to help a team mate. Think before you move – perhaps the best option is to stand still.

Drive and pass off

An attacking player who dribbles past an opponent may not be free to take a shot because a second defender moves across to mark. However, an opportunity has now been created to pass off to the free team mate. This highlights the need for attacking players to be alert and respond to the action of the ball handler, and be prepared to move into a good position to receive a pass (see 'Give and go', page 36).

Post play

A useful move for an attacking player without the ball is a move to the basket, followed by a move towards the ball handler, stopping in a direct line between the team mate and the basket. The stop is made using a jump stop (see page 7) and the ball is received. The passer then cuts (i.e. runs without the ball) close to the new ball handler, trying to force the defender to be obstructed. The player who moves out from the basket to receive the ball is said to be 'posting up'.

Screen play

The type of obstruction caused by the post player in the move above is legal. The obstructing of the movement of the defender is called 'screening' and is commonly used to free an attacking player.

For example, a screen can be for the ball handler to use. If the ball handler still has the dribble to come, another team mate (the screener) can move to stand with one foot either side of an imaginary line that the defender wants to take should the ball handler dribble to the basket. Once the screen is set the player with the ball drives close to the screen, forcing the defender to check his movement to avoid the screen. The dribbling player should now be free to move in for a shot. The screen must remain stationary if the drive occurs, but once the defender's movement has been checked, the screener should move to the basket. This screening action is called a 'pick screen', with the movement of the screener being called a 'roll'. The complete movement is referred to as a 'pick and roll'. If the defenders switch responsibilities, the screener moving to the basket will often be free to receive a pass and shoot.

In addition to the screen being set for the ball handler, it can also be set on a defender marking a player without the ball.

Fast break

Possession of the ball is the difference between being on attack and being on defence. Therefore, the fast break should be an integral part of the attacking play of every team.

In a fast break the team on attack aims to obtain a numerical or positional advantage before its opponents can get their defence organised. The attack should start immediately a team gains possession of the ball. This should be an instant reaction to the change from being the defensive team to being on attack.

Once the team gains the rebound, an outlet pass from the under-basket area should be made. This first move is often made to the side of the court. From here the ball should be passed or dribbled to the middle of the court. Once the ball is in the middle and moving down court, two team mates should join the ball handler so as to create a three-lane attack. The ball may be passed between these players but as the attacking team moves the ball into the scoring area, the ball handler should be in the middle lane – this gives him the opportunity to go all the way to the basket and only pass off when forward progress is blocked.

Defence

Any defensive tactic employed by a team will be based on sound individual defensive skills. An individual's defensive responsibilities are outlined on page 37.

When defending, a team will aim to obtain possession of the ball without the opponents scoring. To achieve this the team will need to do the following two things.

- Defend the high percentage scoring area. This means that any ball handler on attack in this area must be pressured to discourage a shot or to force a poor shot. If an opponent is within an area of court from which they would score a high percentage of any shots taken, then they should be closely marked to prevent pass reception.
- Pressure the ball. The defence should try to take the initiative by attempting to pressure the opponents into errors. The ball handler should be marked, as should potential pass receivers.

Man-to-man defence

The simplest and easiest defensive strategy for a team to play is 'man-to-man' – each defender is assigned to mark a specific opponent regardless of where he goes in his offensive manoeuvres. Defenders will need to concentrate on the opponent rather than the ball. If the attacking opponent is a long way from the basket or the ball, a defender may sag, i.e. move away from his opponent towards the basket he is defending.

Zone defence

In a zone defence all five defenders work as a team unit and react to the ball. In so doing, each is responsible for an area of the court in which he moves in relation to the movement of the ball.

Matching attacking formation

The attacking team will endeavour to dictate where space will occur, in particular by trying to draw defenders from the under-basket area. The defenders should match the formation taken by the attacking team and aim to ensure that the under-basket area is defended.

Communication

Defenders must talk to each other so that they are all aware of attacking moves and defensive commitments. At the simplest level this will involve each player calling out the number of the player he is marking.

Training and practising

When training and practising for basketball it is important that the ball is used as much as possible in the session. The ball should be used not only in passing, shooting and dribbling, but also in defending against ball handlers and potential ball handlers.

Good basketball players will not only need to master the skills and techniques of the game; they will also need to develop a level of physical fitness so that their bodies can cater for the sport's demands.

Physical fitness training will only be effective if demands are made on the body. As the player improves so the demands are increased.

The club coach is responsible for planning and conducting training sessions. During these sessions the coach will organise practices (called 'drills') to enable club members to learn new skills and to develop their present ability. Basketball drills involve repetition of the skill to be developed, and this repetitive nature of club training should form part of the individual training that a player may undertake away from the formal club session.

Shooting practice

It is vital to practise shooting and scoring. The player who is able to fix a basketball ring in his back garden for practice purposes has the potential for considerable improvement.

A useful practice to employ is to start close to the basket, shoot and score. When you score, step one pace back from the basket and shoot again. If this shot scores, step back again; if it misses, step close to the basket and shoot again. This is practising shooting from a spot on the floor that you are fairly certain of scoring from. Vary the directions you step back from the basket after a shot.

With a partner, each take it in turns to shoot a set number of shots (e.g. 10, 20 or 25) and then change round. The shooter's partner collects the rebound and passes the ball to the shooter. The shot can be taken from the spot where the ball is received or following a short dribble.

Whatever shooting practice is employed, it is crucial that a high proportion of the shots taken score – aim to practise *scoring* not missing.

One-on-one

'One-on-one' is an extremely useful drill with which to practise individual offensive and defensive skills.

One player takes the ball from a starting position that is about 4–6 m (15–20 ft) from the basket, with the other player acting as a defender. The attacker tries to score using normal dribbling rules. After each attack the players may change roles or they may decide that while the attacking player scores, he keeps possession and takes the ball back to the starting point to begin a new attack. Alternatively, each player may have a set number of attacks (e.g. 5 or 10) and then they swop over and the new attacker endeavours to better the score of his opponent.

Three-on-three

'Three-on-three' is a training activity that has become an established part of youth basketball; England Basketball now runs national championships for 3v3 at U18, U16 and U14 level.

The game is played in a half-court, into one basket. As its name suggests, each team consists of three players. In a tournament the winning team is usually the first to reach 15 points, with at least a 2-point margin of victory, though this can vary, as can the duration of a game (e.g. ten or 15 minutes).

There are no jump balls. The game starts from out-of-bounds with the team to take the first possession decided by a coin toss between the captains.

Possession changes after each successful field goal, violation of the rules and defensive rebound. On the possession change the ball is 'taken back' to the top of the three-point arc and a new attack is started.

Except for shooting fouls, fouls are penalised by the non-offending team taking the ball out-of-bounds at the side line opposite the top of the three-point arc. Fouls on players in the act of shooting are handled as follows.

● If the basket is made, one additional free throw is awarded to the shooter. Whether this free throw is made or missed, possession goes to the defence.
● If the basket is missed, one free throw only is awarded. If the free throw is scored, the ball goes to the defence; if it is missed, the ball is retained by the attacking team.

There is no conventional line-up at free throws. After a free throw the ball is always brought into play from the side line opposite the top of the three-point arc by the team that was on defence at the free throw.

The three-on-three game gives the opportunity to develop many basic skills of the game.

● Safe passing – you cannot score if you lose possession.
● Moving free to receive the ball – the passer needs a good target to hit with the pass.
● Good shot selection – a player should only take a shot when he is free and confident that he is at a range from which he can score.
● Blocking-out and rebounding – rebounding a missed shot creates more possession of the ball.
● Playing good individual defence against a player with and without the ball.
● Making the basic team plays of drive and pass off, give and go, post play, and screen play (screens can be set on the ball handler's defender and against the defender marking away from the ball).

Fitness training

Basketball involves non-stop action and if players are to succeed they will need to be in good physical condition. Away from club training sessions this could include running 3–4 miles (5–6 km) two or three times each week to establish a degree of basic fitness.

Shuttle runs

Basketball requires quick bursts of speed over a relatively short distance, so shuttle runs should be included in a player's training regime.

The standard markings on the court can be used to measure the length of the shuttles. A player starts and finishes each shuttle at the end line. The first run is to touch the free throw line and back to the end line; followed by to the centre line and back; then to the far free throw line and back; finally, to the far end line and back to the finish. He should sprint at top speed throughout the shuttles and, after a rest period, should complete two or three sets of shuttles during a training session.

Variations of the game

Wheelchair basketball

Wheelchair basketball is played by competitors in wheelchairs under the same rules (with a few simple adaptations), with the same ball and in the same court as the conventional game. The game can be played by anyone, even someone with a minimal physical disability which affects his legs, so long as he can sit in and self-propel a wheelchair. Apart from those with sensory disabilities (e.g. the blind and deaf), wheelchair basketball is played by people from almost all disability groups. It is played by those with polio and cerebral palsy, amputees, paraplegics, and even those with minor mental disabilities. Wheelchair basketball is the only team game in which nearly all physically disabled people can take part and compete on equal terms.

The main differences in the rules concern jump balls, dribbling, progressing with the ball, and the five seconds restriction.

A jump ball is only used at the start of each half. In other jump ball situations teams will alternate in taking possession of the ball for a throw-in from out-of-bounds. The team not gaining control of the ball following the initial jump ball will begin the alternating process.

Dribbling in a wheelchair occurs when a player:

• pushes his chair and bounces the ball simultaneously
• alternately pushes his chair and bounces the ball. The ball shall be placed on the lap (not between the knees) while pushing the chair, and one or two pushes shall be followed by one or more bounces

• uses both of the above sequences alternately.

A 'push' occurs when a player applies forward or backward movement with the hands to one or both wheels.

A player in a wheelchair may progress with the ball in any direction within the following limits.

• The number of pushes while holding the ball shall not exceed two.
• Any pivot movements shall be considered part of the dribble, and limited to two consecutive pushes without bouncing the ball. To progress with the ball in excess of these limits is a violation.

Instead of the three second rule of the running game, in the wheelchair variation the restriction is five seconds.

Mini basketball

Mini basketball is a game for the nine to 12 age group, based on the conventional game.

The major differences between the adult game and mini basketball are the height of the ring (which is 2.60 m/8.53 ft rather than 3.05 m/10 ft above the floor) and size of the ball (which is smaller than a normal basketball – approximately a size 5 soccer ball).

A game is divided into four playing periods of ten minutes. Each member of the team must play at least one ten minute period, and no player may play in all of the first three quarters.

There is no 24-second rule, three point rule, or team foul rule, nor are there time-outs, or bonus free throws after a basket is scored when the player is fouled in the act of shooting.

Further details may be obtained from England Basketball or Mini Basketball England on 01763 243650.

England Basketball

England Basketball publishes, or co-operates with publishers, in a wide range of books and journals (including 'Zone Press' and 'Coach's Clipboard'), official rules manuals on coaching and officiating, and a variety of pamphlets. Details of publications and equipment available by post and further information on the sport are obtainable from:

England Basketball
48 Bradford Road
Stanningley
Leeds
LS28 6DF
tel: 0113 236 1166
fax: 0113 236 1022
e-mail: enquiries@ebbaonline.net
website: www.basketballengland.org.uk

47

Index